On The Train To Hell

Poems of Sadness and Grieving

TOLU' A. AKINYEMI

First published in Great Britain as a
softback original in 2022

Copyright © Tolu' A. Akinyemi
The moral right of the author has been asserted.
All rights reserved.

No part of this publication may be reproduced, stored in a retrieval system, or transmitted, in any form or by any means, without the prior permission in writing of the author, nor be otherwise circulated in any form of binding or cover other than that in which it is published and without a similar condition including this condition being imposed on the subsequent purchaser.

Cover Design: Buzz Designz

Published by 'The Roaring Lion Newcastle'
ISBN: 978-1-913636-42-5
eISBN: 978-1-913636-43-2

Email:
tolu@toluakinyemi.com
author@tolutoludo.com

Website:
www.toluakinyemi.com
www.tolutoludo.com

ALSO, BY Tolu' A. Akinyemi from
The Roaring Lion Newcastle'

"Dead Lions Don't Roar" (A collection of
Poetic Wisdom for the Discerning Series 1)
"Unravel your Hidden Gems" (A collection
of Inspirational and Motivational Essays)
"Dead Dogs Don't Bark" (A collection
of Poetic Wisdom for the Discerning Series 2)
"Dead Cats Don't Meow" (A collection
of Poetic Wisdom for the Discerning Series 3)
"Never Play Games with the Devil"
(A collection of Poems)
"A Booktiful Love" (A collection of Poems)
"Inferno of Silence" (A collection of Short
Stories)
"Black ≠ Inferior" (A collection of Poems)
"Never Marry A Writer" (A collection of Poems)
"Everybody Don Kolomental" (A collection of
Poems)
"I Wear Self-Confidence Like a Second Skin"
(Children's Literature)
"I am Not a Troublemaker" (Children's
Literature)
"Born in Lockdown" (A collection of Poems)
"A god in a Human Body" (A collection of
Poems)
"If You Have To Be Anything, Be Kind"
(Children's Literature)
"City of Lost Memories" (A collection of Poems)
"Awaken Your Inner Lion" (A collection
of Essays)

Dedication

To the memory of Dr. Chinelo Megafu, and other victims of the Abuja-Kaduna train attack who paid the supreme price with their lives. Nigeria failed you.

Acknowledgements

A big thank you to the editors of the journals below, for giving my poems their first abode.

'Nightmare' first appeared in *My Woven Poetry*.

'Let The Dead Forgive' first appeared in *African Writer Magazine*.

All the glory goes to the Lord for the grace, infinite mercies, and the exceptional talent. I'm very grateful.

To my booktiful family, Olabisi, Isaac and Abigail, sincere appreciation for the love and support on my literary journey with a plethora of booktiful highlights. I love you now and always!

Sincere thanks to Jen Campbell for editing this collection of poems and Diane Donovan for a final proofreading.

A final thanks to everyone who has supported me on this journey that keeps unravelling so many booktiful experiences.

Contents

Dust to Dust 3
Ghosts in Scotland 4
Fire of Fury 5
Soul Ties 6
Orphan 7
Suicidal 8
A Poet's Prayer 9
Condolences 10
Mystery 11
Vanity 12
On The Train to Hell 13
Mountain of Fire 14
Reincarnation 15
Ghost Town 16
Empty 17
Stung 18
Fallen Bird 19
Shocked 20
Misery 22
Republic of Guns 23
Black Friday 24
Why, Oh Why! 25
Notes on Grief 26
Fizzling Dreams 27
Etiquette 28
Orange 29
Pitch Dark 30
Tears 31

Nightmare	32
Buried	33
Worship	34
The Colours of Grief	35
Till Death Do Us Part	36
Megalomaniac	37
Unknown Gun Men	38
Headless	39
Wailing	40
Ominous	41
Pray for Me	42
For Girls	44
Heartbreak	45
Disappearance	46
Let The Dead Forgive	47
This Wealth is Not Yours	48
Dreams End at the Door of Death	49
Darkness	50
Just One More Time	51
Let Thy Will Be Done	52
Blasphemy	53
Eerie Silence	54
Larger-Than-Life	55
Fake News	56
I No Longer Have a Home	57
Author's Note	59
Author's Bio	61

POEMS

Dust to Dust

The synonym of death screams cruel fate.
This symphony of grief in my head hums
Melancholy.

Humans | Dust | Memories
The metamorphosis of life into death
Drums into me: leaves me

Colder than ice.
We wear our pain until our hearts
Become a sorrow bed.

Father was first dust
Before Mother's immaculate steel turned
Into iron rust.

As the words reverberate—from dust we come,
To dust we shall return—
Our dreams swirl into the wind.

Ghosts in Scotland

I saw many ghosts in Scotland
Calling my name—
A free pass to hell.

Jailbreak, this solitude of darkness:
The spirit of an old flame wants a companion
In the afterlife.

My body softens like a mashed potato.
I don't want to die
On this lonely ride whilst

Darkness plays a riddle in my mind,
Pulling at the strings of my soul.
By a whisker, I
Escape

From the shackles of the
Ghosts calling for me.

Fire of Fury

Wildfire has turned
The inner chamber of my heart
Into dark soil.

I have so many questions stabbing
At the depths of
My soul

Which leave me sore.

This memory births mirages:

>How do we flip back the pages
>That have made the atmosphere sombre
>
>And our lives shattered bricks?
>My book of lamentations is a deep sea of
>Regret.
>
>And how do I grieve your passing
>Without erupting into a ball of fire?

Soul Ties

Our souls are conjoined twins
                        bonded by a love
that became stillbirth.
        I no longer have random sex

with strangers. Jane's one-night
             stand was her last dance.
My spirit has been
             shackled in the chains
of expired love. This house
         has become a horror scene.

There are strange voices
                          lingering.
I hear imaginary footsteps
       rushing like a spring fountain.

Time and again, the memories
                open like fresh
wounds and I can't
                seem to untangle
from this wreckage
                  in my soul.

Orphan

Like abandoned goods,
We had no pickers.

Father left with no goodbye notes
And Mother's shoulders shrunk
From lifting a cross too heavy to bear.

Last year, mother snapped and   disappeared
Into the void.

Like scattered birds, we found solace
In foster care.

Suicidal

This weight of worry is standing
On weak foundations.

In your city, suicide is an abominable word,
A synonym for the frail.

Depression clouds your thoughts
And taints your mood.

Darkness has made your heart
An empty nest.

Would you pitch life's light into this dark haze,
Which no tempestuous storm can faze?

Would you fight right 'till the end,
Throwing thunder of your own?

A Poet's Prayer

I sit at the window of heaven, speak

A prayer, mouth agape, straight
Into God's ears. I am

Speaking in a foreign language.
I don't want to be a forgotten song.

Wash me with your mercy
Unending.
Paint my hair white.
Snow white, I slice
My veins and release a stream of wisdom.

I want to ascend the hill of life;
Sit on grey chairs
Counting the stars;

Tell folklore stories of mountains and valleys
In this journey of life.

Condolences

The register of   condolence

    Is filled

    With   holes.

The rendition of commiserations

    Is a recurring pattern.

  Condole

    And console.

Grief has no sequence and its ache is

Immeasurable.

        Loss is a broken net

        Which no calming words can

                Mend.

Mystery

Your loss is an upside-down house, buried
Deep, steep, which no soothing words can fill.

The rooms have lost their colours and
Their sounds are in deep slumber.

My fears have grown wings
And tears pierce my veins.

The language of loss wraps itself in eggshells.

The night you vanished
My heart grew blisters from the aches.

My silent moans are a turbulent wind
That rages against the night.

Vanity

On this passage of time
I chased the wind
And before harvest time
The end was nigh.

On The Train to Hell

I don't want to die for a dying nation
With my name forgotten after the rising sun.

I died the night you became an angel.
The terrorists feasted on your soul
Until you became something else altogether.

Your heartfelt prayer that Nigeria
Would not fail you fell on its sands.

We sent you to Heaven decked
Out in angelic regalia.

How do we send you to hell a second time?

Your gruesome demise on the burning train
Was a bitter pill to swallow.

Mountain of Fire

In the morning, I rain an ocean of curses
On unseen forces.

My tongue is a flame on fire, it levels
Mountains until they cave.

I kill imaginary spirits.

These demons cannot waltz through this force
Of nature without getting scorched.

I am a burning furnace.

Three spirits who wrestled with me last night
Have become simple offerings — sacrificial
lambs.

The gods have been sent on a trip to hell,
With no return address.

Reincarnation

The dead are restless in their graves,
Desperate for a second coming.

Last week, I met a girl on Tinder.
We struck a chord, and I asked:

>*So, when did you die?*

Bewildered, she retorted:
>*Are you ghost-hunting?*

But ghost stories are fairy tales.

My brain is awash with reincarnated stories
Of restless ghosts in tombstones, all seeking
New beginnings.

Ghost Town

I was born in a ghost town:
The silence of dreams

And tradition were memorabilia, so
We repeated them like hauntings.

The chorus of emancipation
Is a banshee storm.

This war cannot be won with phantom planes.
Our dreams pirated ghostships.

A chorus of freedom reverberates victory
From the echo chamber of silence.

Empty

In Kaduna, a baby's first cries seared
Heaven's curtains.
This innocence has been watermarked
By rancorous wailing.

A baby's first abode is a nest of evil,
Of terrorists and agonies
That portend danger.

A baby's welcome song
Is hollow and melancholic.
The language of laughter is
A forgotten memory.

A baby's trauma etched on her veins
Is a sign
Of the times.

Stung

The news anchor on Arise Television is
Submerged in emotion for the umpteenth time.

Her mood flip-flops as sandstorms of terror
Sweep through the land.

She sobbed, yesterday. Today, she drowned
In agony, wilting like a riverbed.

Last night, I cried with her. Crying
For my country is a part-time job.

A poet's cry is a call for justice. I cried in
Rhymes
And rhythmic notes, verses, and stanzas

To do what I can to
Quench this cursed fire.

Fallen Bird

Another bird has tumbled
From the sky.

The news anchor says
Over two hundred people departed without a
Sign.

I am a bag of emotions:
My body carries me.

In Kenya, a little boy will no longer know
His mother's love.

In Canada, a little girl will no longer feel
The warmth of her father.

Fallen birds,
These fallen Angels

Are a family that no longer has a name.

Shocked

i

Our President was shocked to the teeth.
They sunk into his bone marrow.
He wallows in shock yesterday, today, and
Tomorrow.

These shocking deaths
Have swept many from this earth.

Our President is immune to the chorus
Of lamentation, one that has turned our towns
Into deserted lands.

His army of advisers are wearied from penning
Dirges occasioned by the cloudbursts of terror
Which have left piles of body bags and
Mass graves.

Our President's shock works like clockwork.

ii

We have been beguiled by the semantics
Of commiserations;
Shock and condemnation from the
Commander-In-Chief
Whose body language speaks in
Strange tongues.

The blood of the innocent has washed every
Fibre of our
Humanity.

Hope hangs on a thread; our future
Has been covered
By the violence of rampaging demons—
Blood-sucking demons.

We pray to God for vengeance, but our
Sanctuaries
Have become death traps
Where we can no longer find solace.

Misery

The cries of the forgotten are screaming
Bedlam.

Our house has creaking walls
From all the hunger pangs

And the arrows of misery pierce us; pierce time
Again and again.

Republic of Guns

Another deranged shooter is hunting souls —
We are on a slippery slope
Heading into new lows.
Schools have become slaughtering labs
And children sacrificial lambs

The Gun is mightier than the pen!
The Gun is weightier than a human life...

This is a republic of guns and untimely death!

Tonight, twenty-one beds lie in a deserted field.
Gun violence is an earthquake of
Swallowed dreams.

Black Friday

Arise News Report: Over Hundreds of Bodies Burnt - Ovieteme George

It was a Black Friday
When death's carnage flung our misery doors
Ajar.

Black market engulfed in
Smoke plumes;
Black bodies
Burnt—
When will we learn?

The skies wear mournful clouds.

This pain has no name.
These death numbers have been whittled in shame.
This is a game
And tomorrow we will cry again.

Why, Oh Why!

The gentle breeze is a sleeping deity.
Oh, death!
Why, oh why?

The veins of grief shimmer.
Oh, death!
Let me cry, cry, cry!

The nights have become shadows and the
Cobwebs of guilt have replaced the
Flowers of my heart.

Oh, death!
Why, oh why?

Was this destiny, or a plot twist in the
Book of life?

Notes on Grief

She was a mockingbird who made Father's
And Mother's passing into incendiary jokes.

Even in grief,
This emptiness clouds it all.

Is there a manual for grief?

Even when the wails are brief, the days
Are stretched and the night's lights envelope

This total darkness.

Fizzling Dreams

Yesterday's dreams have crystallised into
Balls of sadness.

Death's fangs fizzle dreams
And our anger is a bag of bitter sweets.

When Father died
We wept,
Weeping for our dreams which have become
Candle wax.

When he was lowered into the grave
Our dreams became sandcastles.

Etiquette

We are tearing the rulebooks of mourning.
Etiquette is a broken song
And decorum has been translated badly.

This death is a carnival.
We shall feast on its demise

Break bread with clenched teeth
And intoxicate ourselves on fine wine.

We shall toast
And gloat,

As this passing is more than a tea party.

Orange

My tight walls have been ruptured by this
Crushing blow. Anxious streams have overtaken
Sound judgment.

I awaken with rushing blood.

I am losing my legs under the weight of all

These anxious moments.

Pitch Dark

Wear black.

Let sorrow spread
Across your face,

Let it overflow
Into your organs.

We compose ourselves
Only to fall apart;

Sing dirges wrapped in flowers
To send our dead to glorious exits.

This morning
We are mourning

Our dead
Even in this chilling dread

That makes our hearts
Flat.

Wear black.

Tears

The living are disturbing the dead
With storms of wailing.

Anguish is an earthquake.

The doctor's report has thrown the air
Into a surgery of violence;

This flood of pain, this acid rain.

Nightmare

Our dreams morph into nightmares as
Missiles rain onto our roofs.

Home becomes a crumpled island
And we pick up fragments of hope
To journey into strange lands.

The dark skies grieve for us
As our night's light is engulfed by smoke.

We pray to go back in time
But the memory track is broken.

Buried

I buried our friendship last week
On the ocean sand.

I prayed to the sea goddess to wash it away.

A love built on deceit,
Washed by the sea—

That's poetic justice.

Worship

This is a room of worship.
Touch the page; see the walls.

The night you left,
Your building blocks of love
Cleansed the agony of this room.

We won't wash it with ceaseless tears.
We won't tear it all apart.

This death won't be immersed in
Poetic dark arts.

We will worship this room of ours
until we meet again.

The Colours of Grief

Grief stings my soul and I say a prayer
In harmony with you.

Why did you leave without a farewell note?

This eerie silence is killing me;
Is eating me alive.

My bones' numbness embraces still waters.

I remember all your living colours, but now
Paint me black with this brush of mourning,

For I know it will take an eternity
to wring this sadness dry.

Till Death Do Us Part

Close this book of life, with its torn pages.
Dim these lights that break our voices.
Good people have been served up as food for
Hungry gods.

The idiosyncrasies of the fallible
Have dug us a pit
From which their body language is talking.
Their unspoken words have sent many to a
Great beyond.

We are dying under the rubble of bad
Leadership.
The north/south divide is a wide gulf.
The chasm of tribalism has swallowed us.

This amalgamation of doom is a plague.

We soak in this sea of oppression

                              'Till death do us part.

Megalomaniac

The air is colourful tonight
And our bleak future has been traded
For renewed hope.

The tyrant who was a pillar of death
Has been toppled from the earth.

Only death could
Wipe clean his foul odour.

Death snatched an alibi.
An ally of death repaid his debt.

Our oppressor was on fire, extinguished
Before he took us on a journey to perdition.

Unknown Gun Men

The monsters you made are:
        Sucking blood.
        Planting doom.
        Spreading a quantum level of
                      violence.

The monsters you groomed have:
      Grown
       Thorns.

The monsters you made have:
        Whitewashed our land with blood,
        And we cheer on our albatrosses
        to doomsday.

Headless

If cruelty was a man,
I would laminate it with the insignia of
Unknown spirits:

Black men with darkened hearts
Maiming their own flesh and blood.

Rinse and repeat-
Black men with black hearts
Feasting in a carnival of violence and
Bloodletting.

We won't scream racial injustice-
These unknown monsters have washed
Our land
With a flood of pain

And our walls crack by this sheer force of
Terror sweeping
Throughout the land.

Wailing

We are wailing for the dead,
Moaning and
Mourning.

Our hues and cries crack the skies.
We will disturb the soil
And the men who have lain in it forever.

The dead might be taking notes.
Bloodied eyes are our artifacts of everything.

We will wail like defeated men
And climax on this hill
That has made us a dam of water and
Broken records.

Ominous

Ominous clouds gather for the umpteenth
Time.
The alarm bells dancing are a dark sign.

Our evil seeds hatch to amplify a
Bloodbath of anarchy and pillage — why

Has this clandestine assembly
Birthed such an orgy of violence?

Pray for Me

"I'm on the train. I have been shot, please pray for me." - Chinelo Megafu

Would you pray for me in this duel
Of destruction — my life a disappearing cloud?

Would you pray for me as I gasp for air
And death overshadows me?

When my phone beeps and messages are
Running riot?
When my body is waxed cold?

Would you pray?

Terrorists' bullets have made this body an
Empty hole
But these torrents of hate snapped
All that was left.

"Are you dead yet?" a waste of sperm asked.

Another retorted, "You pathetic liar!"

While another organism laughed in derision:
"Hahaha."

I am a shattered poet.

We shall bookmark their tweets for generations to come.
We shall reprint these IDIOCIES in BOLD fonts.

Would you pray?
Would you pray?
Would you pray?

For Girls

Today, I woke up crying
For girls who have no other name but
Endurance.

For girls who bloom
Into gloomy women.

For girls who have been watermarked
With the label of 'unwanted.'

For girls whose innocence has been tainted
With cruelty.

For girls who carry alphabets of
Unspoken words.

For girls whose agonies spread
Like stretch marks.

For girls everywhere, with scars that sting.

Heartbreak

"Ukraine war: The heart-breaking moment Ukrainian children with cancer are forced to say goodbye to their fathers and flee." - Sky News

Needless wars swept us farther
From our fathers.

Children are fighting unseen wars in their
Bodies.
They soldier on in the midst of this
Calamitous rain.

The ego of this monster has sent us to the
Brink of extinction.

We call on the spirit of vengeance:
Wash away our enemies before dawn
So we can enjoy the twilight of our lives.

Disappearance

The news tunnelled into my heart.
Desolation stings like bees.

Yesterday, your laughter: a shining lantern.
Today, your life: a closed chapter.

Why did you become a rain cloud?

I woke up today dishevelled,
My chest burdened with all this weather.

I tried to piece together the memory of you
But it has become the fragments of an
Unravelled puzzle.

Why did you choose to leave?
You'd promised yourself to me.

You have become the wind.
My life now is a horror film.

Let The Dead Forgive

I have sent emissaries to the land of the dead,
But my letters have remained unread.

I have laid wreathes at your tombstone
But my heart cannot move on.

I wish I could send you off with bliss and laughter;
Enrapture you with obsessive love.

Alas, your memory of me was snaked
With pain. Let the dead forgive,

Let the dead forgive!

Please, leave me to grieve
And live in peace.

This Wealth is Not Yours

Father walks the slopes of life with wobbly legs
'Till he reaches the summit.

Give him life, and a new song.
Give him hymns
Of joy unfettered.

A billionaire's son is praying for his
Father's demise.
His exit meal ticket is a pack of falling cards.

Father ascends the totem pole of life.
In health
And in wealth.

A son's prayer is a stench that reeks of
Atrocious calamity.

Dreams End at the Door of Death

Dreams are piling up at the door,
At the door of death.

Dreams are ashes at the door,
At the door of death.

Dreams are wax at the door,
At the door of death.

This death trap traps hopes
In forgotten hymns
At the door of death.

We walk on anguished mountains
At the door of death.

And our dreams are valleys of dust
At the door of death.

We have become wailing wailers
At the door of death

Where evil is lurking and knocking
At the door of death.

And our lives disappear with the wind
At the door of death

Where this debt
Hangs like a heavy cross
At the door of death.

Darkness

i

Darkness spreads its wings
And good men are rotten fruits.

Like solaced stars
We are burning lamps

Burning this earth with a beam of light.

ii

Tonight, the wind is crying.

We are solemn in the quaking earth.

The earth harvests the dark
And hope erases every shadow.

Just One More Time

Why did you fly on the wing of angels
With promises like unopened
Christmas presents?

Why did you leave before sunset,
Before your defrosted spring?

And my skin is falling off
And I have cried and cried

For I want to see you just one more time

To:

>   Baptize you with love,
>   Share communion with your spirit,
>   Serenade you with affection.

One last time...

Let Thy Will Be Done

I will die on this hill
For your will, alone.

The winds of April
Leave me ill.

Gusts crush my skeleton,
Bones and sinew all undone.

Tonight, my hands caress the sea.
Lead me to the land of the free.

Refill me with oil afresh.
Grill me;
Distill me for your glory
And let thy will be done.

Blasphemy

For Deborah Samuel, who was accused of blasphemy, stoned to death, and burnt to ashes by Northern Muslim students of the Shehu Shagari College of Education, Sokoto State, Nigeria, on May 12, 2022.

I never wanted to share a country with
People

>Who bay for blood
>For their God.

Paint it with the sound bite: sacrilege!

A young woman has been railroaded
By bloodthirsty bigots
Who wallow in barbarism.

Let's watermark this ignorance
With polluted education.

Let our God fight!
Let our God fight!
Let our gods right
This wrong: make this torrid night

The end of this vicious cycle that makes
Christians
Burnt offerings on these altars of sacrifice.

Eerie Silence

Written on May 13, 2022, after Arise News reporters failed to discuss the death of Deborah Samuel after airing a commentary of the incident on Trending with Ojy Okpe on The Morning Show. The commentary was later deleted on their YouTube channel after a backlash.

Yesterday, a Christian girl was stoned to death.
An effigy of
Ashes...

Today, the truth died.
Your silence sliced the air and
We choked on it.

Your selective amnesia spoke volumes —
In the newsroom, morality was exiled.

We are swimming in the sea of cowardice.

Death to free speech!
Death to free speech!

Daring journalism is a cliché.

Who will bail us out of these doldrums?
Who will release us from this abusive marriage
Before we drown?

Larger-Than-Life

Former vice-president of Nigeria Atiku Abubakar deleted his condolence tweet to Christian student Deborah Samuel, who was murdered by Northern Muslim youths for blasphemy, after he was threatened by Northern voters, and later distanced himself with another post on Facebook, written in the Hausa language.
"There cannot be a justification for such gruesome murder. Deborah Yakubu was murdered, and all those behind her death must be brought to justice.
"My condolences to her family and friends." – Atiku Abubakar

Today, I wept for my sinking
Country, brimming with rotten egg politicians.

Justice is now an orphaned child —
The ghosts of persecuted Christians are crying-
Crying for vengeance.

Today, your larger-than-life ambition was
Buried in the sea.

This uprising of evil birthed on the altar of
Political correctness is a ticking, ticking

Bomb.

Fake News

TVC News reporters tried to whitewash the death of Deborah Samuel by spreading misinformation about her death, linking it to the strike embarked upon by the Academic Staff Union of Universities.
The TV station later apologised for the error in their report.

TVC News is owned by APC Presidential Candidate Bola Ahmed Tinubu.

The truth is on trial
And we dance with the fire
Of misinformation.

This spreading erosion;
This tangled oppression.

Our conscience has grown blisters and
The foundation of truth is built on quick

Sand. And this cup of desolation hangs
Like dark clouds.

This death will not be coloured with
Falsehoods

Or whitewashed
By selfish politicians and their media tools.

I No Longer Have a Home

I no longer have a home-
A refuge on these lonely nights.

I no longer have a heart-
It has been swallowed by a mighty

Groundswell of evil.

Can you see the trauma etched into my face?

I no longer have emotions-
They have been swept into the sea

Oh, won't you take my weathered hand and
please follow me?

Author's Note

Thank you for the time you have taken to read this book. I hope you enjoyed the poems in it.

If you loved the book and have a minute to spare, I would appreciate a short review on the page or site where you bought it. I greatly appreciate your help in promoting my work. Reviews from readers like you make a huge difference in helping new readers choose a book.

Thank you!
Tolu' A. Akinyemi

Author's Bio

Tolu' A. Akinyemi (also known as Tolutoludo & the Lion of Newcastle) is a multiple award-winning author in the genres of poetry, short stories, children's literature, and essays. His works include Dead Lions Don't Roar (poetry, 2017); Unravel Your Hidden Gems (essays, 2018); Dead Dogs Don't Bark (poetry, 2018); Dead Cats Don't Meow (poetry, 2019); Never Play Games With the Devil (poetry, 2019); Inferno of Silence (short stories, 2020); A Booktiful Love (poetry, 2020); Black ≠ Inferior (poetry, 2021); Never Marry a Writer (poetry, 2021); Everybody Don Kolomental (poetry, 2021); I Wear Self-Confidence Like a Second Skin (children's literature, 2021); I Am Not a Troublemaker (children's literature, 2021); Born in Lockdown (poetry, 2021); A god in a Human Body (poetry, 2022); If You Have To Be Anything, Be Kind (children's literature, 2022); City of Lost Memories, (poetry, 2022); Awaken Your Inner Lion, (essays, 2022); On The Train To Hell, (poetry, 2022); You Need More Than Dreams (poetry, forthcoming – January 2023); and The Morning Cloud is Empty (poetry, forthcoming – March 2023).

A former headline act at Great Northern Slam, Havering Literary Festival, Crossing The Tyne Festival, and Feltonbury Arts and Music Festival, he also inspires large audiences through spoken word performances and has appeared as a keynote speaker in major forums and events. He facilitates creative writing master classes for many audiences.

His poems have appeared (or are forthcoming) in the 57th issue (Volume 15, No. 1) of the Wilderness House Literary Review; The Writers Cafe Magazine Issue 18; GN Books; Lion and Lilac; Agape Review; Continue the Voice; My Woven Poetry; Black Moon Magazine; Calla Press; Football in Poetry 2 Anthology; and elsewhere.

His poems have been translated into Greek.

He was appointed as a columnist for 2022 in Malimbe Magazine (Malimbe is the official in-flight magazine of several Nigerian Airlines, including Arik Air, Aero Contractors, Dana Air, and Bristow). Their monthly edition has a readership coverage of 500,000 readers on over 1,600 flights connecting 30 plus cities.

His books are based on a deep reality and often reflect relationships and life, featuring people he has met in his journey as a writer. His books have inspired many people to improve their performances and/or their circumstances. Tolu' has taken his poetry to the stage, performing his written word at many events. Through his writing and these performances, he supports business leaders, other aspiring authors, and people of all ages who are interested in reading and writing. Sales of the books have allowed Tolu' donate to charity, allowing him to make a difference where he feels it's important and showing that he lives by the words he puts to page.

He is a co-founder of Lion and Lilac, a UK-based arts organisation, and sits on the board of many organisations.

Tolu' is a financial crime consultant as well as a Certified Anti-Money Laundering Specialist (CAMS) with extensive experience working with leading investment banks and consultancy firms.

He is a trained economist from Ekiti State University (formerly known as University of Ado-Ekiti (UNAD)).

He sat for his master's degree in Accounting and Financial Management at the University of Hertfordshire, Hatfield, United Kingdom.

Tolu' was a student ambassador at the University of Hertfordshire, Hatfield, representing the university in major forums and engaging with young people during various assignments.

Tolu' Akinyemi was born in Ado-Ekiti, Nigeria and lives in the United Kingdom. Tolu' is an ardent supporter of Chelsea Football Club in London.

You can connect with Tolu' on his various social media accounts:

Instagram: @ToluToludo
Facebook: facebook.com/toluaakinyemi
Twitter: @ToluAkinyemi | @ToluToludo

www.ingramcontent.com/pod-product-compliance
Lightning Source LLC
Chambersburg PA
CBHW030310100526

44590CB00012B/585